Dinosaurs

Joseph Staunton and Luis Rey

W
FRANKLIN WATTS
LONDON • SYDNEY

Contents

A world of dinosaurs

The world we live in is around 4.5 billion years old. Scientists know that there has been life on Earth for around 3.6 billion years because of **fossils** they have found. Some of these fossils were creatures called dinosaurs.

The age of the dinosaurs

Dinosaurs were the most famous group of animals to exist in **prehistoric** times. They were the largest land-living creatures that have ever lived. Alongside them lived many smaller, bird-like dinosaurs, monsters of the oceans and massive flying **reptiles**. We know about these creatures because of the fossil remains they left behind. Dinosaurs lived in different **periods** of time, shown in the timelines in this book.

A changing world

The Earth at the beginning of the age of the dinosaurs was very different from how it looks now. It was made up of one big **supercontinent** called **Pangea**.

Dinosaurs evolved and spread out across this supercontinent during the **Triassic** period. That is why fossils of the same type of dinosaurs can be found around the edges of the continents. Dinosaurs lived by the seaside, on river banks and in desert **oases** during Triassic times, and grazed on the branches of trees such as **conifers**. In the **Jurassic** period, the **climate** got milder and moister, and more dinosaurs started to appear.

Triassic world Most of Earth's land is joined together in a single supercontinent.

Cretaceous world The supercontinent starts to split up.

Cretaceous changes

Over time, Pangea began to split up and dinosaurs started to change. By the end of the **Cretaceous** period, the dinosaurs that lived in North America looked very different from those in South America, and those in Europe, Asia and Africa. **Vegetation** changed, too. Flowering plants sprung up all over the world, and different types of dinosaurs able to eat these evolved.

Destruction!

Then, 65 million years ago, the dinosaurs were quite suddenly all wiped out.

Scientists think that this may have been caused by the impact of an enormous **meteor** that struck in Mexico. The only dinosaurs that survived were the bird-like (**avian**) dinosaurs, who were able to burrow, swim or dive to escape the catastrophic effects of the meteor impact. After the dinosaurs came a new age – the age of the **mammals** (and that includes people).

Dinosaur timeline

This timeline shows the periods from the Devonian to the Cretaceous, and when the different dinosaurs were alive.

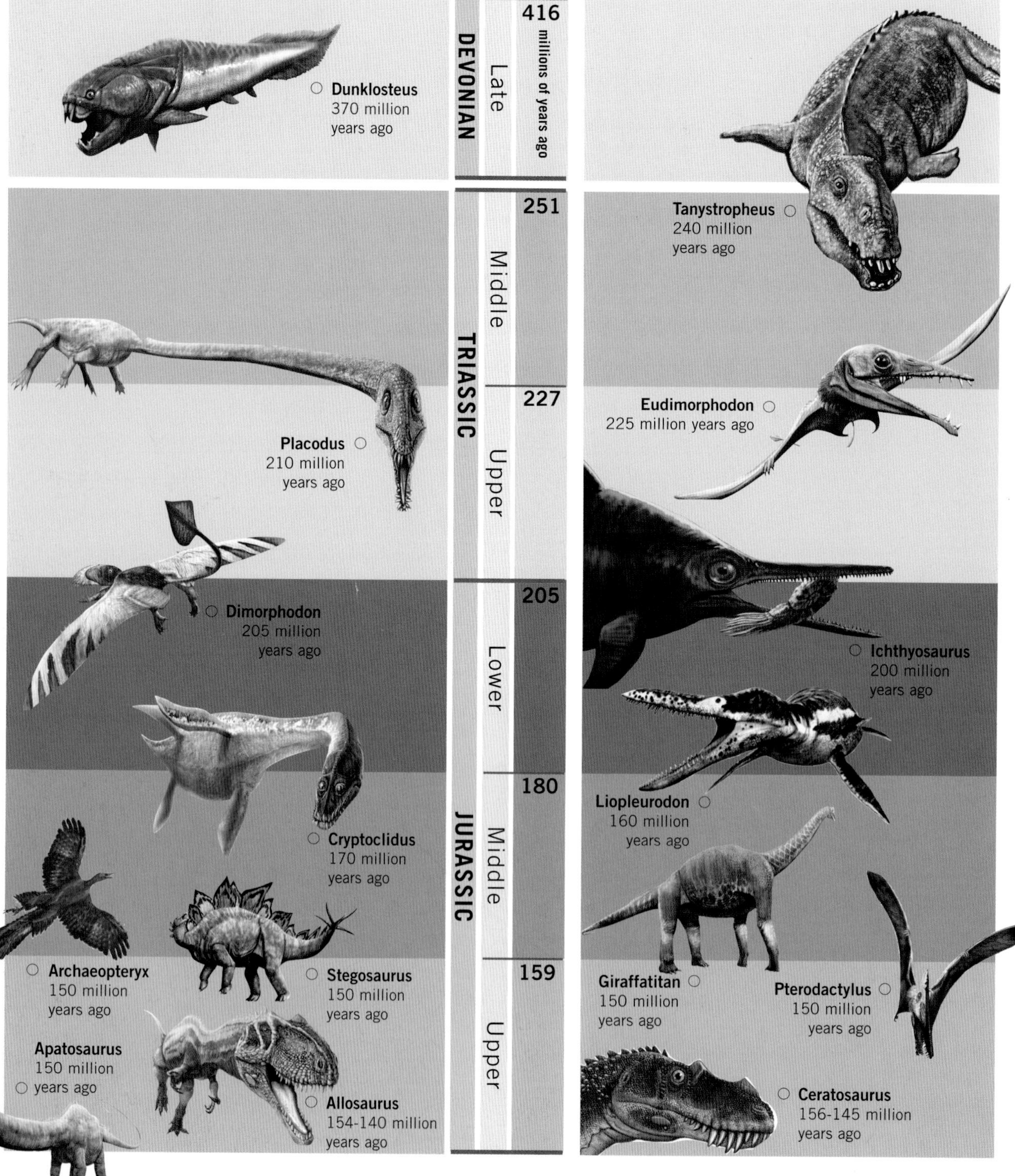

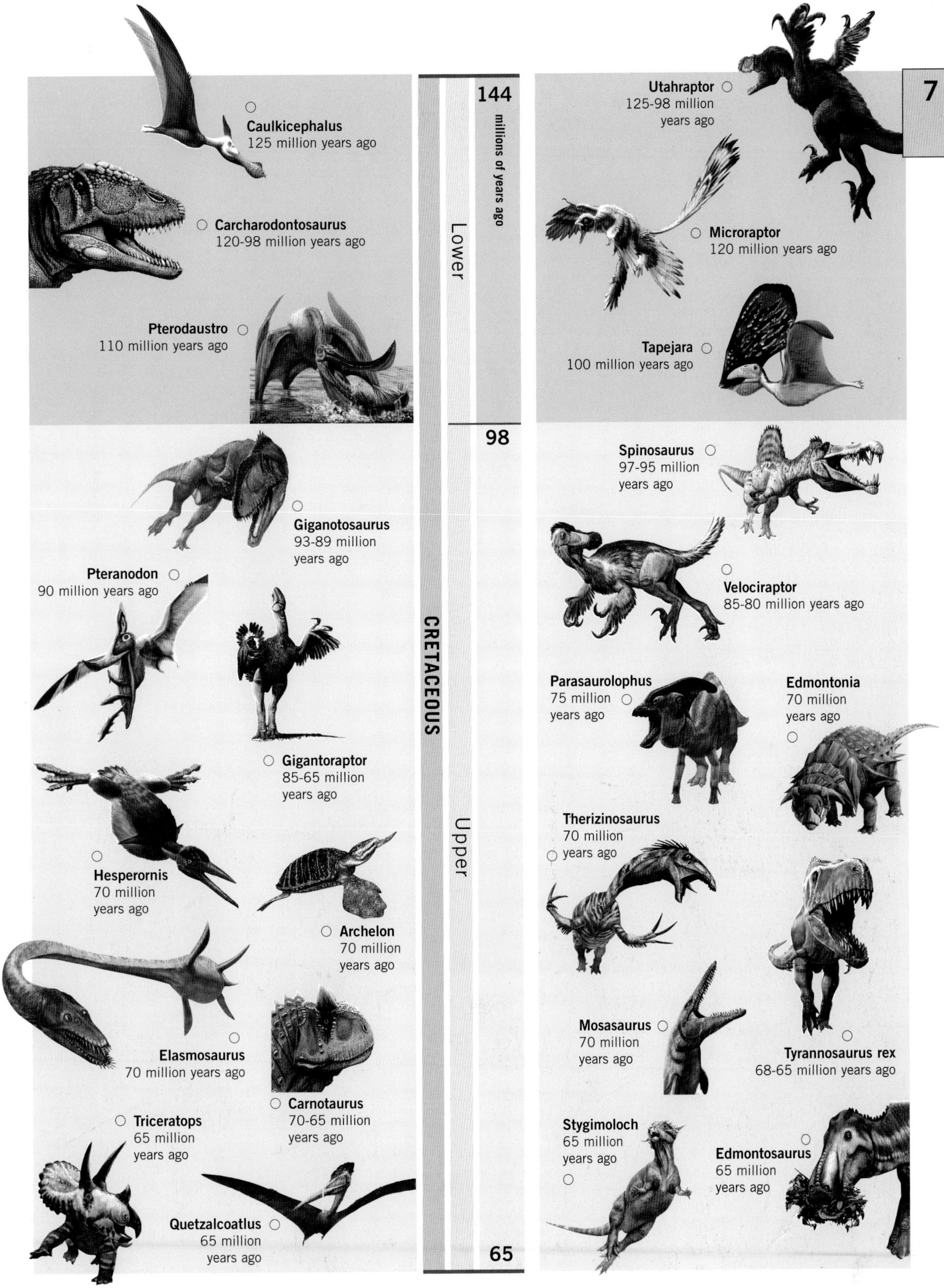

144

millions of years ago

Lower

98

CRETACEOUS

Upper

65

Caulkicephalus
125 million years ago

Carcharodontosaurus
120-98 million years ago

Pterodaustro
110 million years ago

Utahraptor
125-98 million years ago

Microraptor
120 million years ago

Tapejara
100 million years ago

Giganotosaurus
93-89 million years ago

Pteranodon
90 million years ago

Gigantoraptor
85-65 million years ago

Hesperornis
70 million years ago

Archelon
70 million years ago

Elasmosaurus
70 million years ago

Carnotaurus
70-65 million years ago

Triceratops
65 million years ago

Quetzalcoatlus
65 million years ago

Spinosaurus
97-95 million years ago

Velociraptor
85-80 million years ago

Parasaurolophus
75 million years ago

Edmontonia
70 million years ago

Therizinosaurus
70 million years ago

Mosasaurus
70 million years ago

Tyrannosaurus rex
68-65 million years ago

Stygimoloch
65 million years ago

Edmontosaurus
65 million years ago

Giraffatitan

Giraffatitan (arm lizard) was a giant ***sauropod*** that lived in Africa during the late Jurassic period. It was one of the largest animals ever to walk the Earth. It gets its name because of the fact that its 'arms' were longer than its legs.

PREDATORS

A healthy adult *Giraffatitan* probably had no **predators**, because of its size. The largest-known meat eater of that time was *Allosaurus* (pictured far right), which was less than half the size of this gentle giant.

Dino-Data

Height	8 metres
Length	25 metres
Weight	54,500 kg

NECK

Giraffatitan used its long neck to reach up and chop off the tops of tall trees. It swallowed its food whole, without chewing it.

SENSE OF SMELL

Giraffatitan had nostrils on the top of its head, and large nasal passages. This means that it probably had an excellent sense of smell, perfect for sniffing out the juiciest leaves.

Agustinia

Agustinia (Agustinia lizard) was a heavily armoured dinosaur that lived during the early Cretaceous period in South America. Its fossils were discovered in Argentina in 1997.

ARMOUR

Agustinia had spikes and plates running right down the centre of its back. Some soared to heights of nearly 2 metres. Agustinia would probably have used its armour to scare off predators and attract **mates**.

RARE SPECIES

Only a few parts of this dinosaur have been found by fossil hunters. They include bones from the back, hips, legs and tail, and nine of Agustinia's amazing plates and spikes.

Dino-Data	
Height	4.5 metres
Length	15 metres
Weight	4,072 kg

Edmontonia

Edmontonia (lizard from Edmonton) was a huge, tank-like dinosaur that lived during the late Cretaceous period. It was one of the last armoured dinosaurs on Earth. Fossilised skeletons have been found in Canada.

Dino-Data

Height	2 metres
Length	7 metres
Weight	4,000 kg 

TERRITORY

Male *Edmontonia* fought with other males for **territory** and mates. Bigger males used their large shoulder spines for shoving contests.

DIET

Edmontonia had pouches in its cheeks, used for storing food. It also had a sharp beak that it used to slice through tough plant material.

ARMOUR

This creature wore the perfect defence for protection from **carnivores** – body armour! It was covered from head to toe with spikes and plates. Its only weakness was its soft belly.

Apatosaurus

Apatosaurus (deceptive lizard) was one of the longest animals ever to walk the Earth. It lived during the late Jurassic period in North America, and was a slow, lumbering giant.

TAIL

If any animal was brave enough to attack *Apatosaurus*, it would be making a big mistake. This dinosaur could defend itself by using its long tail as an enormous whip.

Dino-Data

Height	3 metres
Length	23 metres
Weight	22,680 kg

NECK

Some people think *Apatosaurus* used its 12-metre-long neck to graze across large areas of vegetation. Others think that it poked up into the top of trees to reach fresh leaves.

Edmontosaurus

Edmontosaurus (Edmonton lizard) was a large, duck-billed plant eater that lived during the late Cretaceous period in Alberta, Canada. It was a slow-moving dinosaur that would have been constantly threatened by hungry meat eaters.

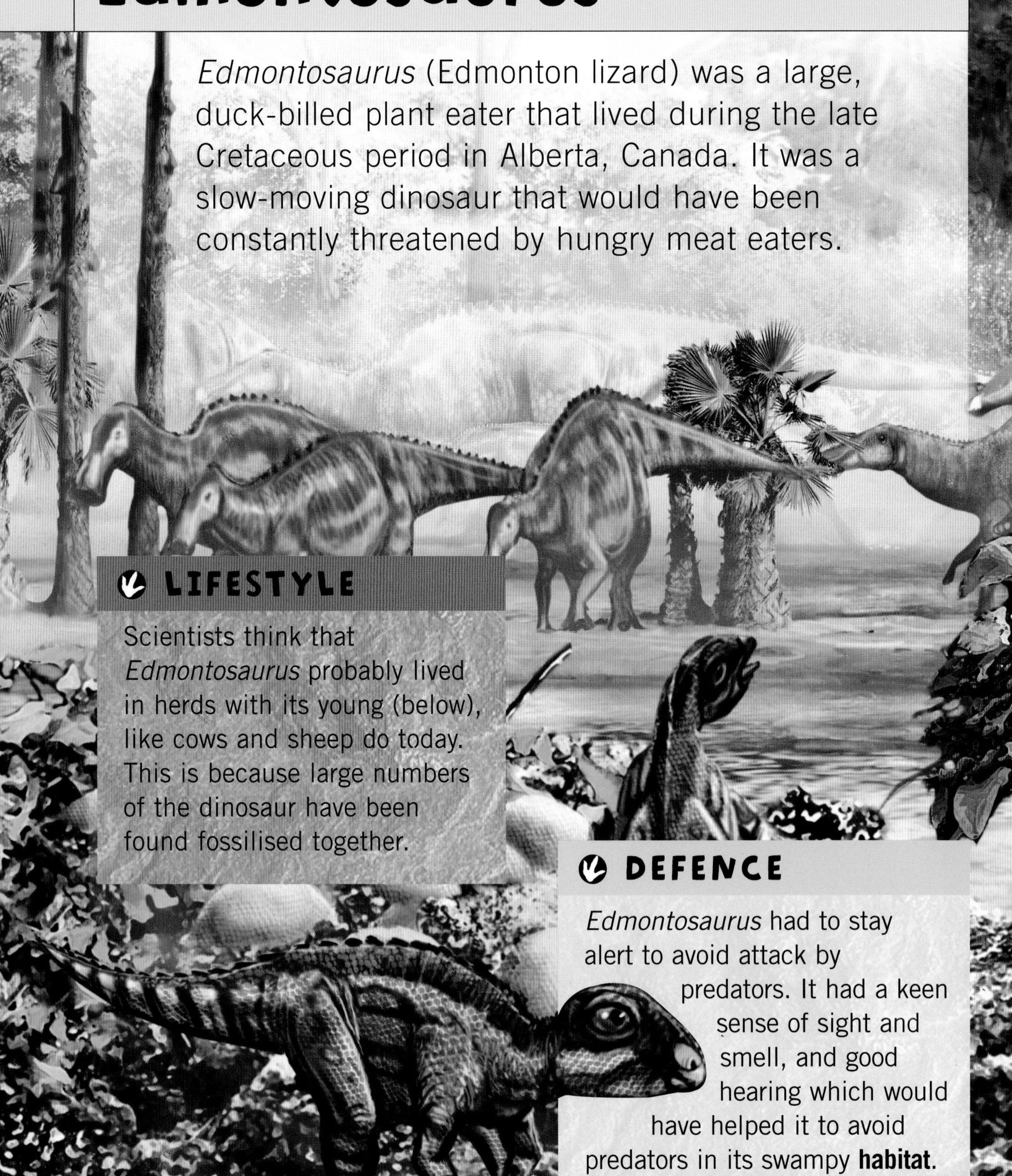

LIFESTYLE

Scientists think that *Edmontosaurus* probably lived in herds with its young (below), like cows and sheep do today. This is because large numbers of the dinosaur have been found fossilised together.

DEFENCE

Edmontosaurus had to stay alert to avoid attack by predators. It had a keen sense of sight and smell, and good hearing which would have helped it to avoid predators in its swampy **habitat**.

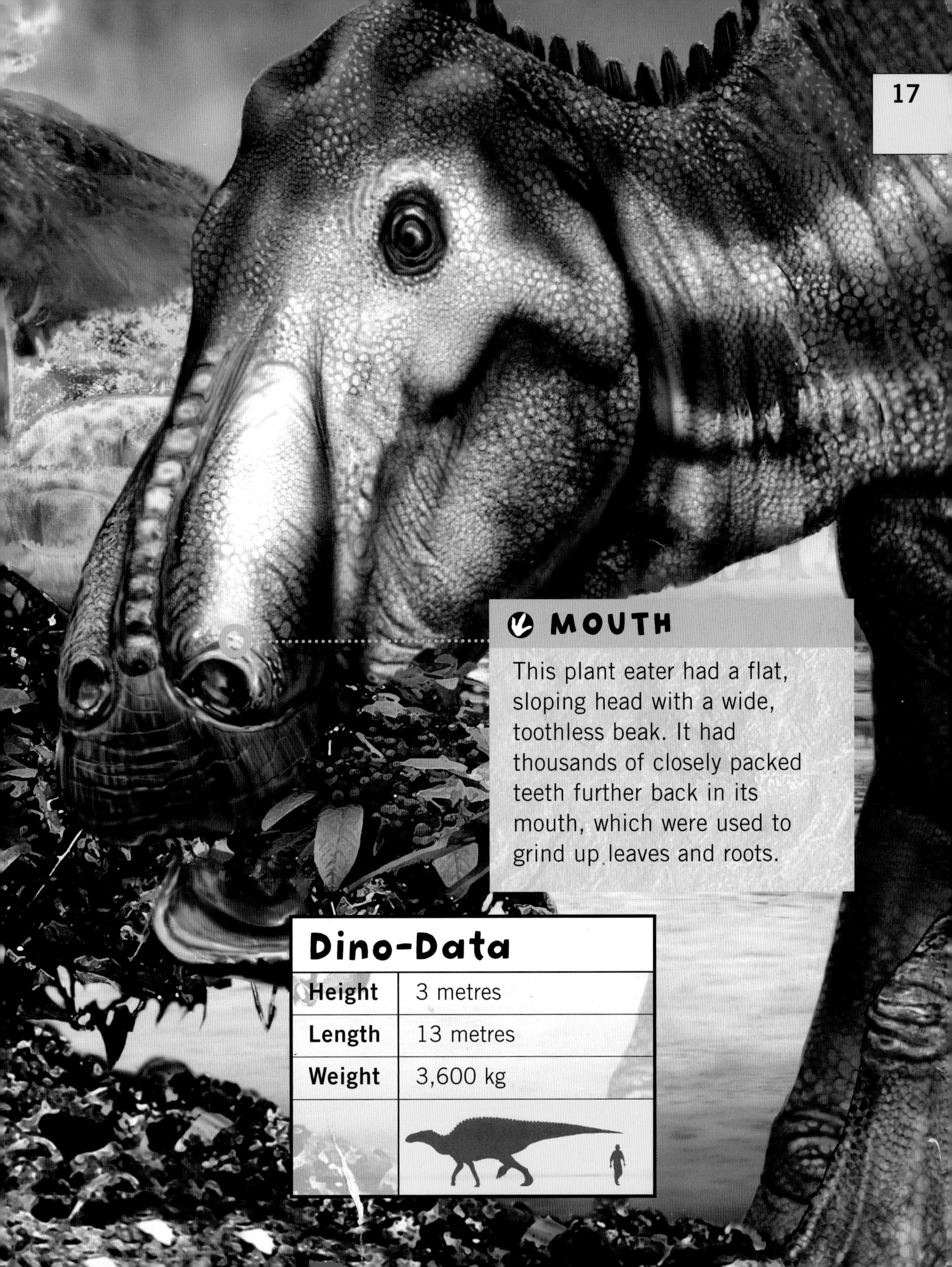

MOUTH

This plant eater had a flat, sloping head with a wide, toothless beak. It had thousands of closely packed teeth further back in its mouth, which were used to grind up leaves and roots.

Dino-Data

Height	3 metres
Length	13 metres
Weight	3,600 kg

Parasaurolophus

Parasaurolophus (crested lizard) was a duck-billed dinosaur with a striking bony crest on the top of its head. It lived in North America during the late Cretaceous period.

MOVEMENT

From the moment it was born, *Parasaurolophus* walked and ran on two legs, and could move quite quickly. It dropped to all fours to eat, and may have also spent some time in the water.

Dino-Data

Height	3 metres
Length	13 metres
Weight	3,600 kg

CREST

Parasaurolophus's hollow crest was nearly 2 metres long. It was probably used to attract a mate, and may even have been able to make a sound a bit like a foghorn.

DIET

Scientists have found fossilised *Parasaurolophus* stomachs. They show that this dinosaur ate a **diet** of pine needles, leaves and twigs.

Stegosaurus

Stegosaurus (covered lizard) was a plated dinosaur that lived in western North America during the late Jurassic period. It was a heavily built creature, about the size of a bus.

PLATES

Stegosaurus had between 14–22 bony plates running down its back. They may have been used to stop the dinosaur getting too hot or cold, or perhaps to attract a mate by changing colour.

TAIL

Stegosaurus had giant spikes at the end of its flexible tail. These would have made an excellent weapon to fight off predators such as this *Allosaurus* (left).

Dino-Data

Height	4 metres
Length	9 metres
Weight	2,000 kg

BRAIN

Stegosaurus had a very tiny brain – about the size of a walnut. This is very small in relation to the size of the dinosaur, and meant that this dinosaur was extremely low in intelligence.

Therizinosaurus

Therizinosaurus (scythe lizard) lived in the late Cretaceous period in Mongolia. When the first fossils were found in 1940, scientists thought they belonged to a giant turtle. When more remains were discovered, however, it was obvious that they belonged to a much stranger creature.

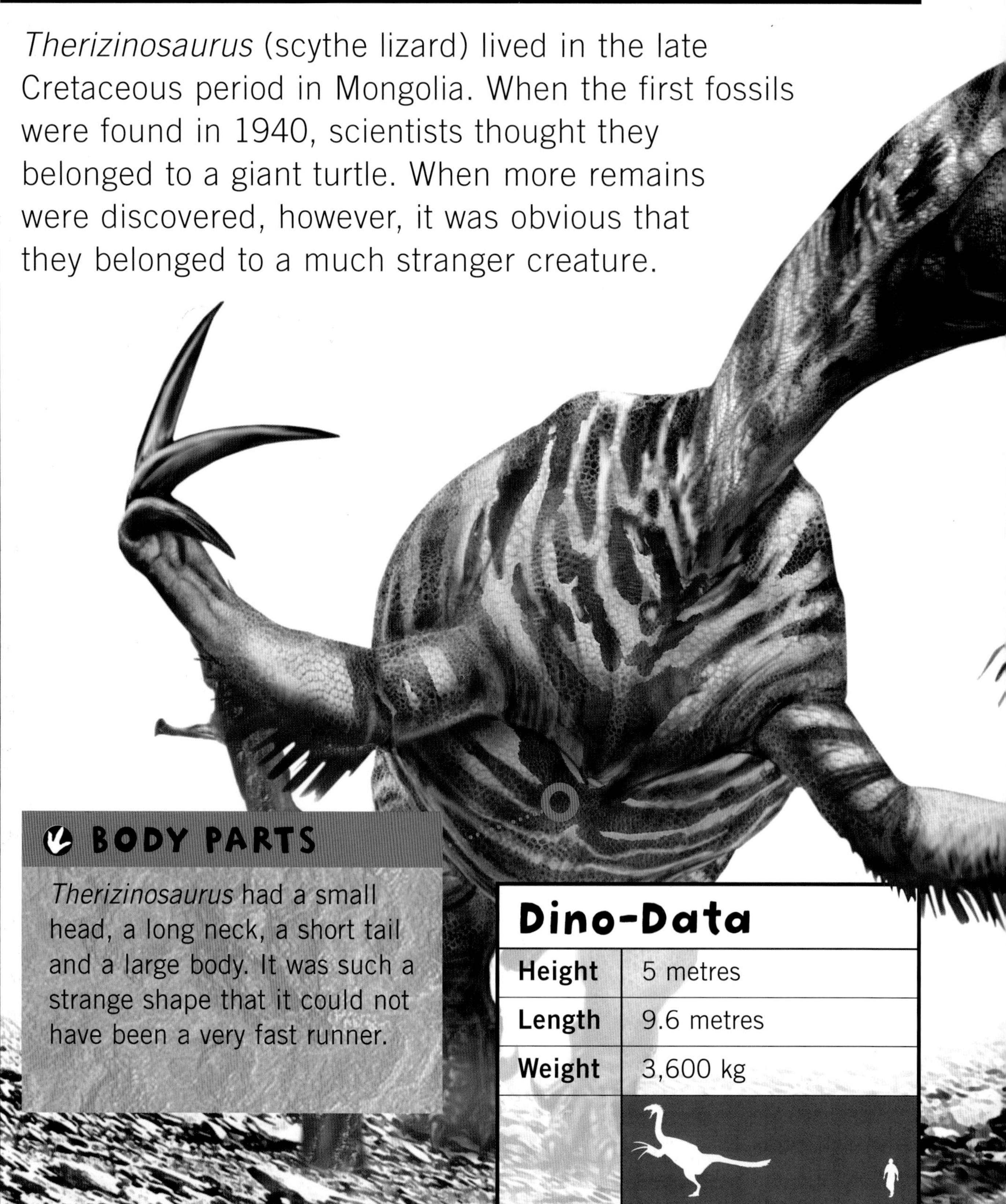

BODY PARTS

Therizinosaurus had a small head, a long neck, a short tail and a large body. It was such a strange shape that it could not have been a very fast runner.

Dino-Data

Height	5 metres
Length	9.6 metres
Weight	3,600 kg

DIET

Despite its frightening appearance, *Therizinosaurus* was just a plant eater. It used its monstrous claws to strip bark and push leaves into its mouth.

MIGHTY CLAWS

Therizinosaurus had three gigantic claws on each of its hands. They probably grew up to one metre in length. They would have been used to warn off any possible predators.

Triceratops

Triceratops (three-horned face) was a rhinoceros-like creature that lived in North America during the late Cretaceous period. It was one of the last dinosaurs ever to live on Earth.

BIG HEAD

Triceratops had a 2-metre long skull, one of the largest of any land animal. Its enormous head was nearly a third of the size of its body.

Dino-Data

Height	2.9 metres
Length	7.9 metres
Weight	5,500 kg

DEFENCE

Triceratops had a giant head frill. This protected its neck from attack from dinosaurs such as this ***Tyrannosaurus***. It was brightly coloured to make the animal look big and fierce from the front.

Stygimoloch

Stygimoloch (horned devil from the river of death) lived at the end of the Cretaceous period. It roamed alongside *Tyrannosaurus* and *Triceratops* in the Western United States. In 1995, a complete skeleton of this dinosaur was found.

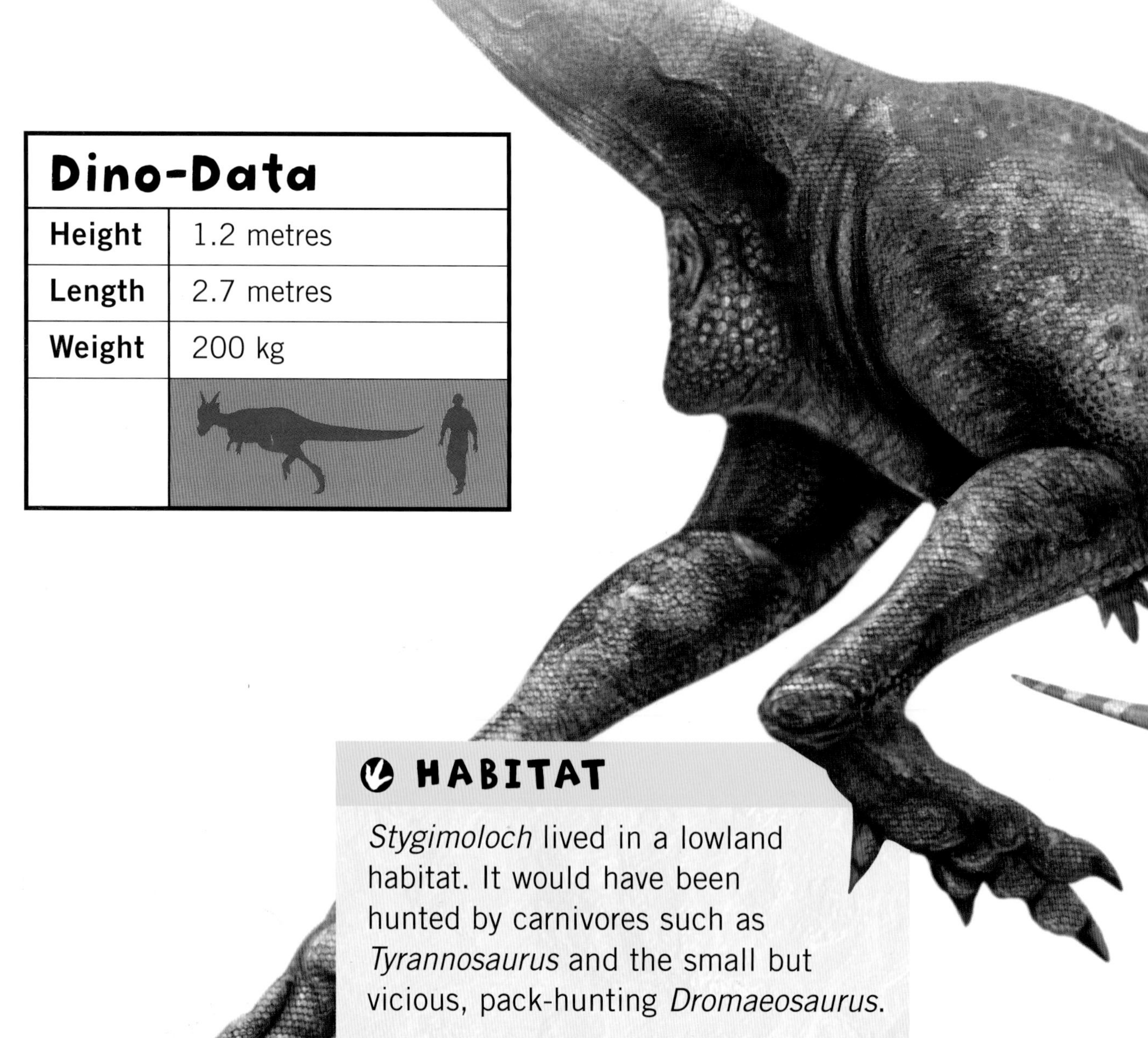

Dino-Data	
Height	1.2 metres
Length	2.7 metres
Weight	200 kg

HABITAT

Stygimoloch lived in a lowland habitat. It would have been hunted by carnivores such as *Tyrannosaurus* and the small but vicious, pack-hunting *Dromaeosaurus*.

HEAD BUTT

In the past, people thought male *Stygimoloch* used their heads as battering rams to fight off predators. Today, scientists think they were used to joust with other *Stygimoloch* for female attention, like stags do today.

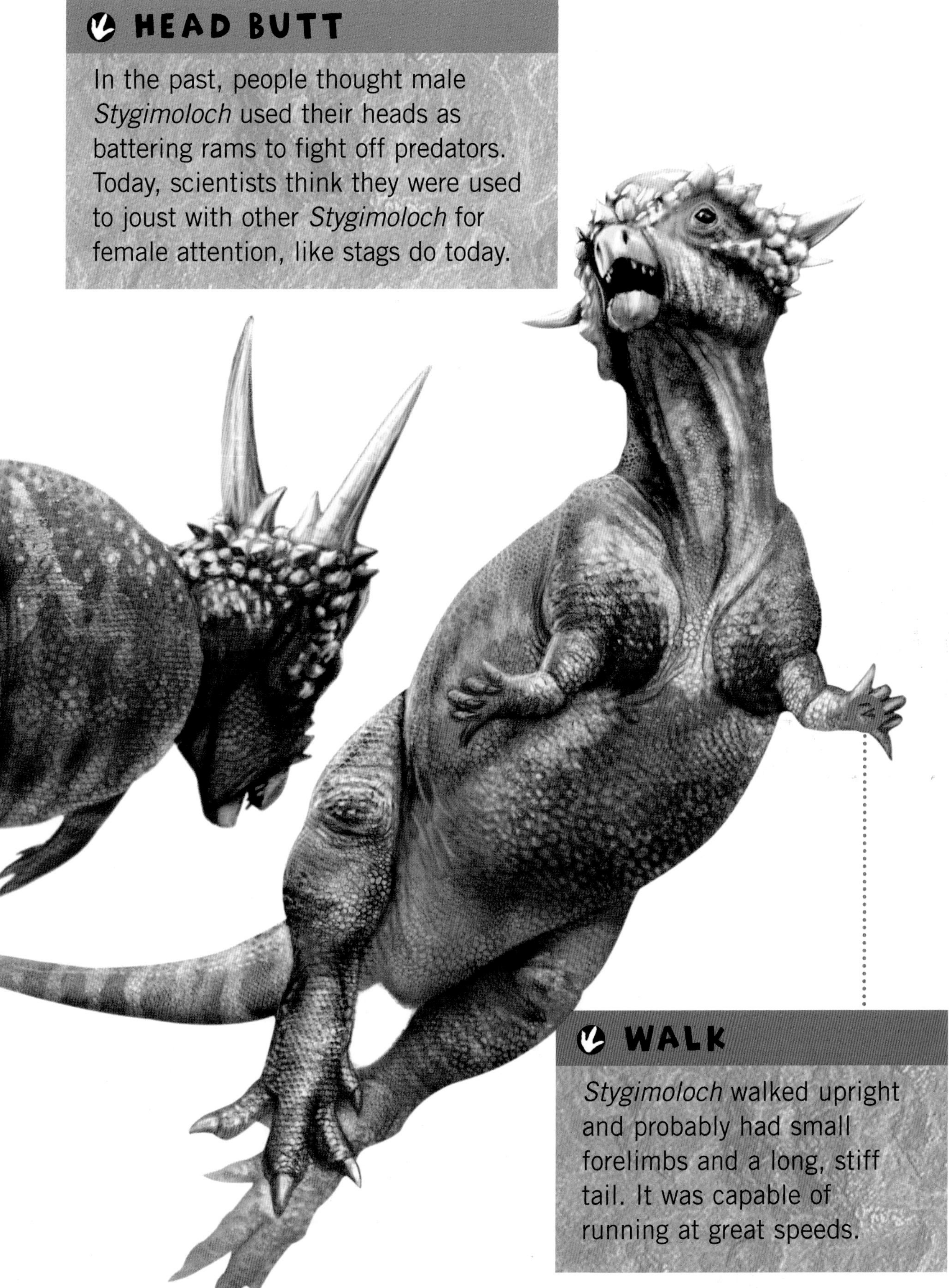

WALK

Stygimoloch walked upright and probably had small forelimbs and a long, stiff tail. It was capable of running at great speeds.

Tyrannosaurus rex

Tyrannosaurus rex (tyrant lizard king) was the king of the dinosaurs. As tall as a house, quick and armed with a deadly bite, it was one of the most scary animals ever to walk the Earth.

LEGS

T-rex's legs were long and powerful. It was fast for such a big animal, but many smaller dinosaurs would have been quick enough to escape this monster.

FOOD

With its banana-sized teeth and bone-crushing bite, *T-rex* ate large herbivores such as this *Alamosaurus* (centre). T-rex, a cretaceous carnivore, also feasted on the remains of dead dinosaurs.

Dino-Data

Height	4 metres
Length	12.8 metres
Weight	6,800 kg

Allosaurus

Allosaurus (different lizard) was one of largest carnivores of the Jurassic period. It was lightly built, but very powerful. Its fossils have been found across the Western United States, and also in Portugal.

CLAWS

Allosaurus had three fingers on each hand, each with huge claws. These 25-cm weapons were used to rip into the flesh of other dinosaurs.

Dino-Data

Height	4 metres
Length	9.7 metres
Weight	2,300 kg

FOOD

As well as eating smaller animals, *Allosaurus* also hunted in packs to catch giant herbivores called sauropods.

TEETH

This carnivore had huge jaws with blade-like teeth to slice up meat. If a tooth broke, another one grew back in its place.

Carcharodontosaurus

Carcharodontosaurus (shark-toothed lizard) was a gigantic carnivorous dinosaur that lived during the Cretaceous period. Fossils of this dinosaur have been found in North Africa. They show that its body was even longer than that of *Tyrannosaurus rex* (see pages 28-9).

SKULL

Carcharodontosaurus had long, sharp teeth and a huge skull. Despite this, though, it was not intelligent. It had a much smaller brain than *T-rex*.

Dino-Data

Height	7 metres
Length	13.5 metres
Weight	7,258 kg

BALANCE

This North African dinosaur had a thick-set body, heavy bones and a massive tail, which it used for balance. It could lumber after and catch big herbivores like this *Paralititan*.

Giganotosaurus

Giganotosaurus (giant southern lizard) is the biggest meat eater ever discovered. It lived during the Cretaceous period. *Giganotosaurus* fossils were first found by a car mechanic in Argentina whose hobby was looking for dinosaur bones!

MOVEMENT

Giganotosaurus walked on two legs, and could move at speed. Its slim, pointed tail was used to provide balance and make quick turns while running.

FOOD

Fossils of big plant eaters called **titanosaurs** have been found near *Giganotosaurus* remains. This suggests this meat eater's diet included giant herbivores.

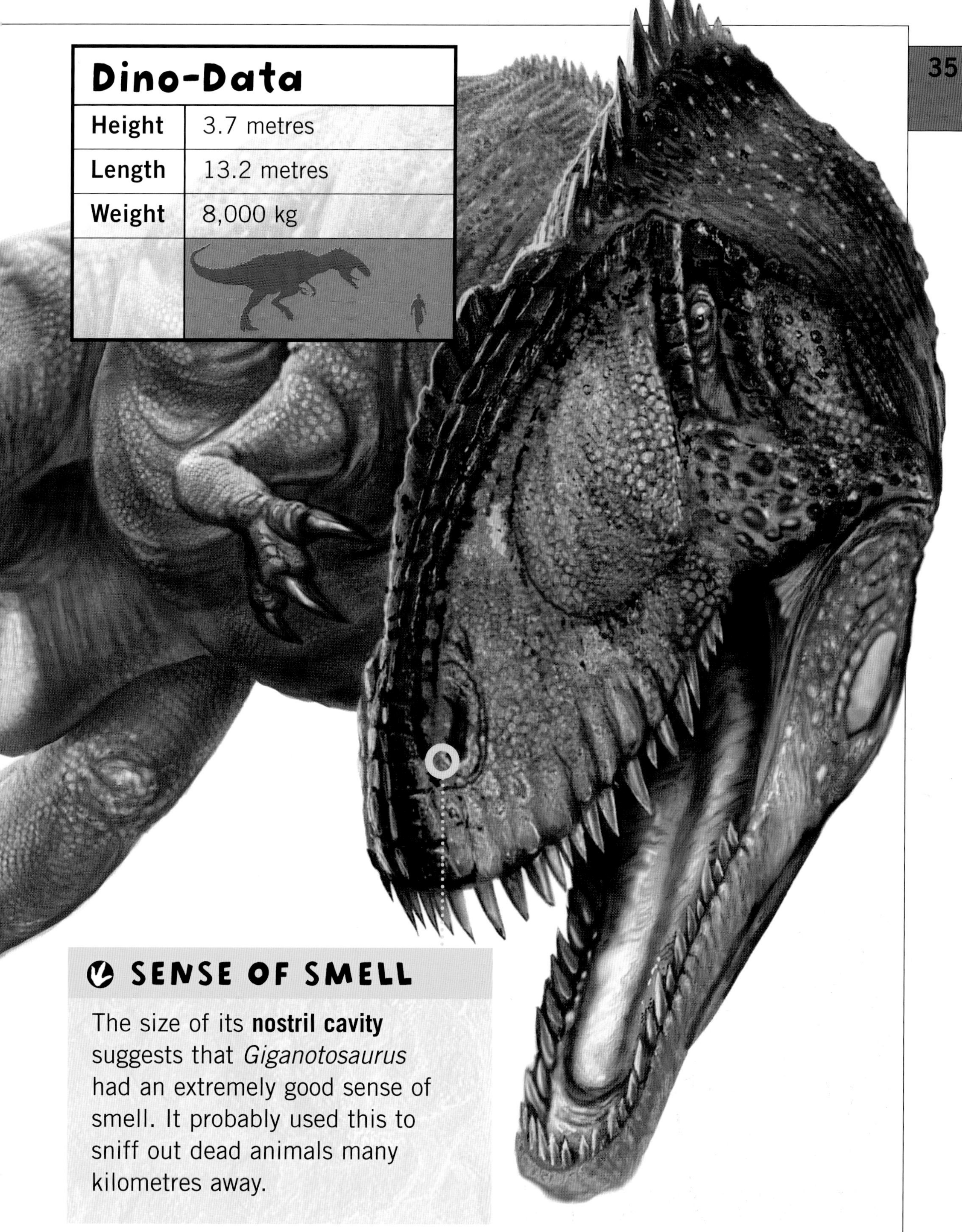

Dino-Data

Height	3.7 metres
Length	13.2 metres
Weight	8,000 kg

SENSE OF SMELL

The size of its **nostril cavity** suggests that *Giganotosaurus* had an extremely good sense of smell. It probably used this to sniff out dead animals many kilometres away.

Carnotaurus

Carnotaurus (carnivorous bull) was a large meat-eating dinosaur that lived during the Cretaceous period. A single fossilized skeleton was found in Argentina in 1985.

Dino-Data

Height	4 metres
Length	7.5 metres
Weight	1,600 kg

HORNS

Carnotaurus had two thick horns above the eyes. It would probably have used these to fight with other males for the attention of a mate.

SKIN

The *Carnotaurus* fossil shows that this dinosaur had skin lined with rows of bumps. It might have been able to change its appearance to blend in with the surroundings, like a chameleon.

Spinosaurus

Spinosaurus (spine lizard) lived in North Africa during the Cretaceous Period. The first remains found of this dinosaur were destroyed in World War II (1939-1945), but parts of its skull have been discovered in recent years.

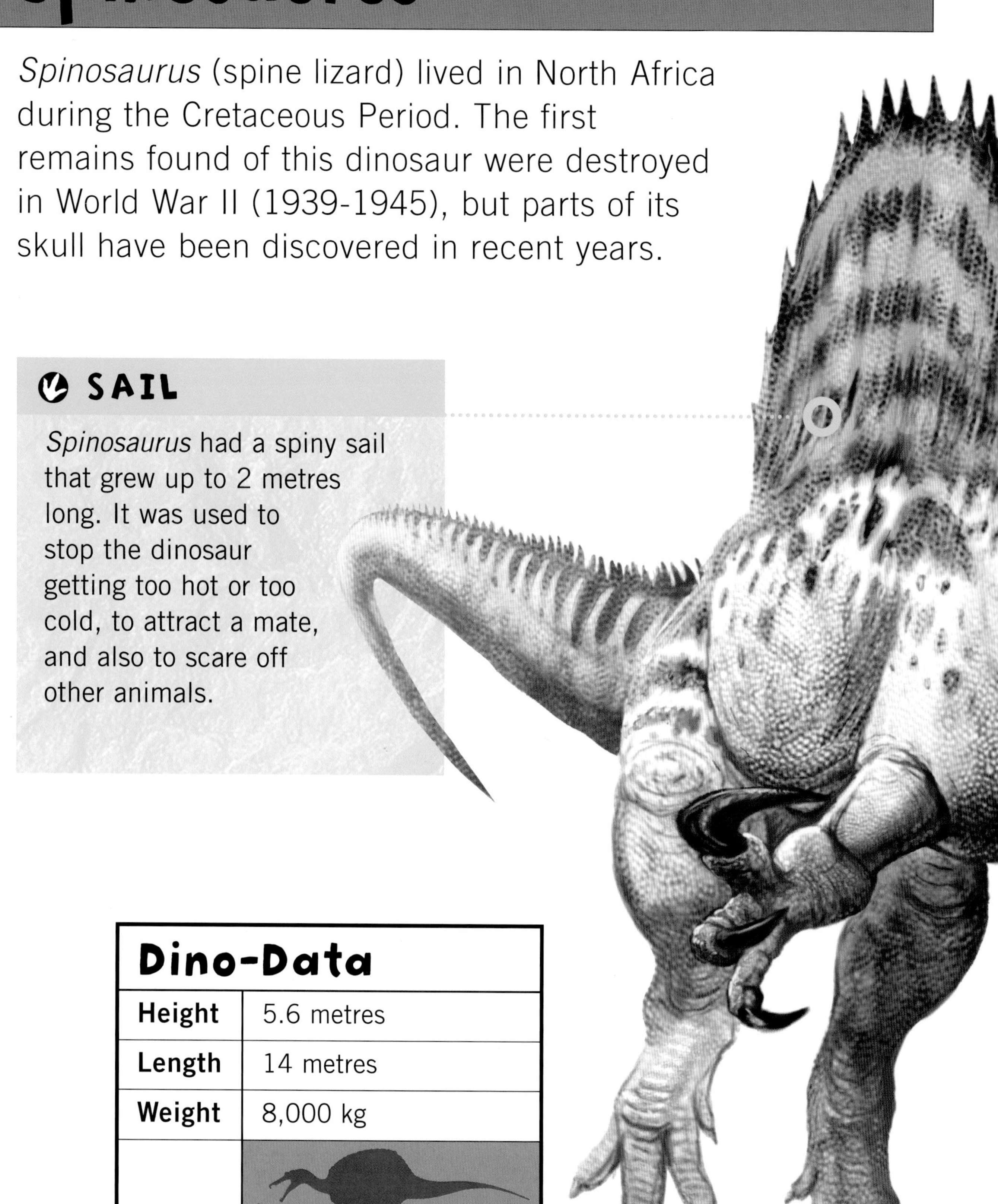

SAIL

Spinosaurus had a spiny sail that grew up to 2 metres long. It was used to stop the dinosaur getting too hot or too cold, to attract a mate, and also to scare off other animals.

Dino-Data	
Height	5.6 metres
Length	14 metres
Weight	8,000 kg

HEAD

The skull had a narrow snout filled with straight, smooth teeth. These were perfect for eating fish with.

CLAWS

Spinosaurus had a diet a bit like that of a grizzly bear. It would have used its long, sharp claws to hook fish out of the water. It also feasted on smaller dinosaurs, and the remains of dead animals.

Utahraptor

Utahraptor (hunter of Utah) was a terrifying Cretaceous meat eater. Its fossils have been found in the United States. It was a lightly built, speedy, bird-like dinosaur.

LETHAL WEAPONS

Utahraptor had a huge curved claw on its second toe that could grow to 23 centimetres long. It hunted by grasping its **prey** with its front legs while kicking at it with its back legs.

HUNTER

Utahraptor's long tail was used for balance and fast turning ability. Here it has hunted down a heavily armoured plant eater called a *Gastonia*, ready for a fight to the death.

Dino-Data

Height	2 metres
Length	7 metres
Weight	700 kg

Ceratosaurus

Ceratosaurus (horned lizard) was a large meat eater from the Late Jurassic Period. Its fossils have been found in North America, Tanzania and Portugal.

FOOD

Ceratosaurus had a flexible body with a tail shaped like a crocodile's. This means it would have been a good swimmer and probably ate a fish-based diet.

Dino-Data	
Height	2.5 metres
Length	8 metres
Weight	1,000 kg

HEAD

Ceratosaurus had large jaws, dagger-like teeth and a blade-like horn on its snout. It had large eyes, which gave it good eyesight which allowed it to track prey from a distance.

Gigantoraptor

Gigantoraptor (giant thief) was a huge, bird-like dinosaur that lived in Mongolia, near China, during the Cretaceous Period. It looked similar to a turkey – but 35 times bigger! This monster was larger than the tyrannosaur *Alectrosaurus* (below), and would not have been easily frightened.

Dino-Data

Height	5 metres
Length	8 metres
Weight	1,400 kg

APPEARANCE

Gigantoraptor had a beak instead of toothed jaws. It probably had feathers too, and hatched eggs in the same way that modern birds do.

FOOD

Gigantoraptor had powerful back legs that allowed it to chase after its prey, and large, slashing claws that it could have used to rip into flesh.

Velociraptor

Velociraptor (swift hunter) was a ferocious, feathered meat eater. It lived during the Cretaceous period in Mongolia.

JAWS

Velociraptor had 28 teeth on each side. They were jagged at the back, making it easier to snatch and hold on to fast moving prey.

INTELLIGENCE

Velociraptor had one of the biggest brains relative to its size out of all the dinosaurs. This intelligent, cunning creature probably hunted in packs, and may have killed very large dinosaurs.

Dino-Data	
Height	1 metre
Length	2 metres
Weight	15 kg
	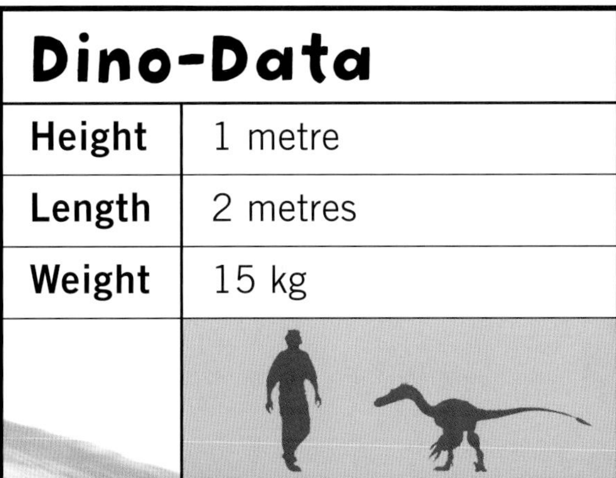

KILLING CLAWS

Velociraptor had a huge, curved claw on each back foot. This seven-centimetre weapon was used to slash at other animals, while the claws on its hands gripped onto the prey.

Caulkicephalus

Caulkicephalus (caulk head) was first discovered on a small island off Britain, called the Isle of Wight. A skeleton, teeth and part of the bird's skull were discovered in 1997.

Dino-Data

Wingspan	2 metres
Weight	1.5 kg
Length	1 metre

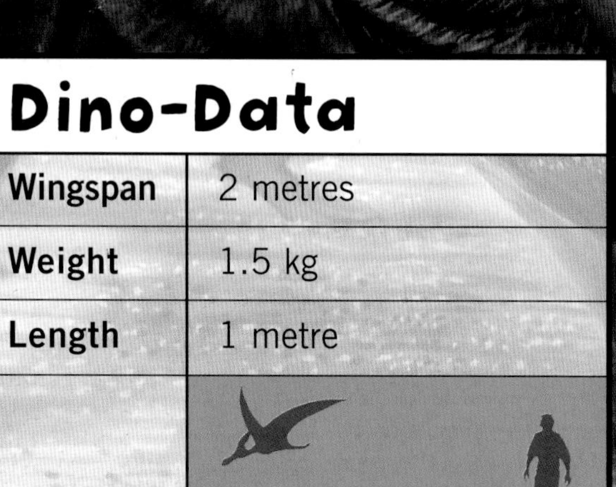

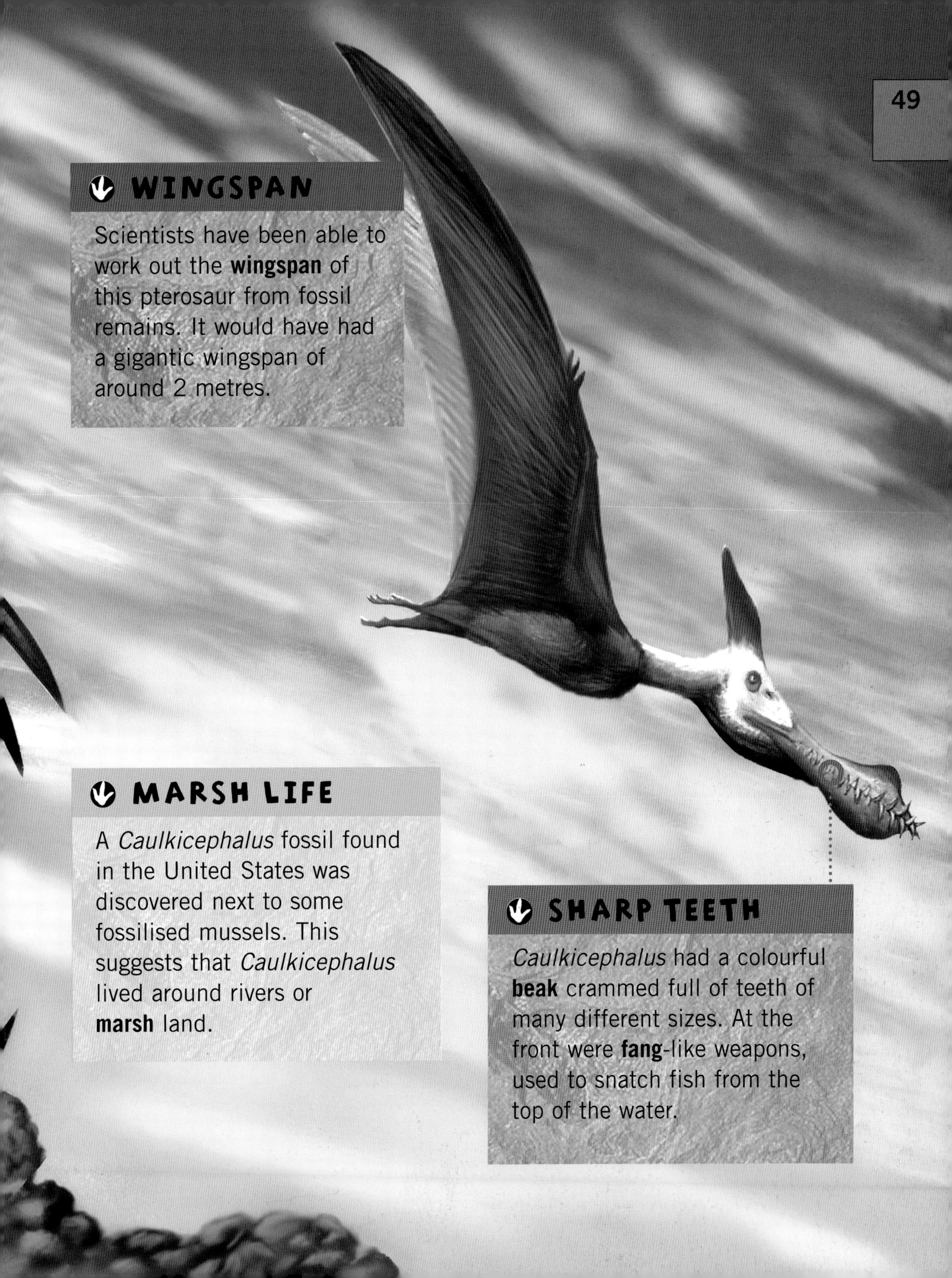

WINGSPAN

Scientists have been able to work out the **wingspan** of this pterosaur from fossil remains. It would have had a gigantic wingspan of around 2 metres.

MARSH LIFE

A *Caulkicephalus* fossil found in the United States was discovered next to some fossilised mussels. This suggests that *Caulkicephalus* lived around rivers or **marsh** land.

SHARP TEETH

Caulkicephalus had a colourful **beak** crammed full of teeth of many different sizes. At the front were **fang**-like weapons, used to snatch fish from the top of the water.

Archaeopteryx

Archaeopteryx (ancient wing) is the earliest and most **primitive** bird known. About the size of a magpie, the first complete **specimen** was discovered in 1861. This bird lived in the Late Jurassic Period on islands that make up modern Germany.

LIKE A DINOSAUR?

Despite looking like a bird, *Archaeopteryx* had more in common with small dinosaurs. It had jaws with sharp teeth, a long, bony tail and deadly claws on its **forelimbs**.

Dino-Data	
Wingspan	0.3 metres
Weight	500 grams
Length	0.5 metres

FIRST FEATHERS

Fossils of *Archaeopteryx have* been found showing impressions of feathers. They suggest that *Archaeopteryx* was the first flying bird, and a link between dinosaurs and modern birds.

HUNTER

Archaeopteryx had long legs and large feet, which suggest it spent much of its time on the ground. It probably searched for food in trees, shrubs and open ground, seizing small prey with its jaws or claws.

Eudimorphodon

Eudimorphodon (true *Dimorphodon*) was a flying reptile that lived in the Upper Triassic Period. It is one of the earliest pterosaurs to have existed. The first example was discovered by Mario Pandolfi near Bergamo, Italy, in 1973.

STEERING

At the end of its long bony tail *Eudimorphodon* had a diamond-shaped flap. This may have been used to change direction while *Eudimorphodon* was in flight.

Dino-Data

Wingspan	1 metre
Weight	0.5 kg
Length	60 cm

WINGS

Eudimorphodon, with a wingspan of one metre, was one of the largest Triassic pterosaurs. Experts think it may have had the ability to flap its primitive wings to soar through the air.

TEETH

Eudimorphodon had over 100 teeth packed into a jaw only 6 cm long. The front teeth faced outwards while the back ones had tiny hooks facing in opposite directions, ideal for hooking prey from the water.

Dimorphodon

Dimorphodon (two-formed teeth) was a medium-sized pterosaur from the Lower Jurassic Period. It was named by **paleontologist** Richard Owen in 1859.

BIG HEAD

Dimorphodon had a huge head for its size. It was 22 cm long, with deep, toothed jaws, that would have looked a bit like the beak of a puffin. Its size may have been used by the male to compete for female attention.

Dino-Data

Wingspan	1.2 metres
Weight	0.48 kg
Length	0.6 metres

EARLY FIND

The first *Dimorphodon* fossil remains were found in England by Mary Anning, at Lyme Regis in Dorset in 1828. This region of Britain is now a **World Heritage Site**, and is known as the Jurassic Coast.

CLUMSY LEGS

Like most other pterosaurs, *Dimorphodon's* legs sprawled out at the sides. This meant that it would have been clumsy on land. Instead of walking about when not flying, perhaps it hung from cliffs or branches using its claws.

Quetzalcoatlus

Quetzalcoatlus (named after the Aztec feathered serpent god, Quetzalcoatl) was a pterosaur from the Late Cretaceous Period. It lived in North America and was one of the largest-known flying animals of all time. The first fossils were discovered in Texas in 1971.

LIGHT FLIGHT

Quetzalcoatlus had a wingspan of nearly 11 metres. Despite its size, however, it probably weighed only about 86 kg. It had hollow bones and a small body, with a long, elegant neck and slender jaws.

ALL FOURS

Although *Quetzalcoatlus* spent time soaring through the sky, scientists think it also spent a lot of time on all fours on the ground. It may have hunted in this way too, like herons do today.

BIG BEAK

Quetzalcoatlus belonged to a family of pterosaurs called the *Azhdarchidae*. This group were all toothless, and had long, thin beaks and stiff necks up to 3 metres long.

Dino-Data

Wingspan	11 metres
Weight	86 kg
Length	5 metres

Tapejara

Tapejara (old one) was a Brazilian pterosaur that lived during the Cretaceous Period. Its most striking feature was its huge and brightly coloured crest.

SIZE

There were many different **species** of *Tapejara*. *Tapejara imperator* was the largest, with a wingspan of up to 6 metres.

Dino-Data

Wingspan	6 metres
Weight	9 kg
Length	Up to 6 metres

CURVED BEAK

Tapejara had a beak that curved downwards. Experts think it used this to pluck fish from the sea.

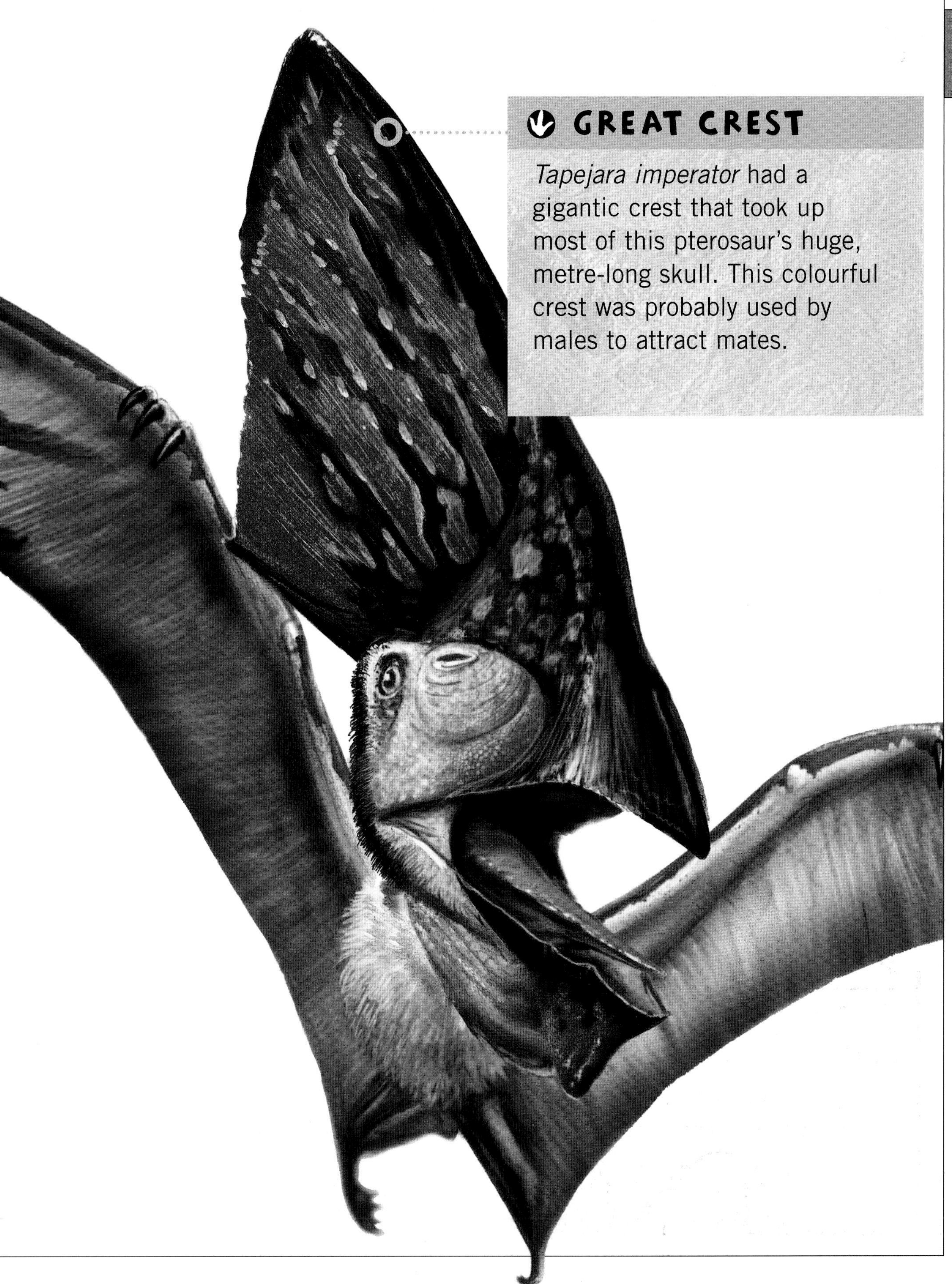

GREAT CREST

Tapejara imperator had a gigantic crest that took up most of this pterosaur's huge, metre-long skull. This colourful crest was probably used by males to attract mates.

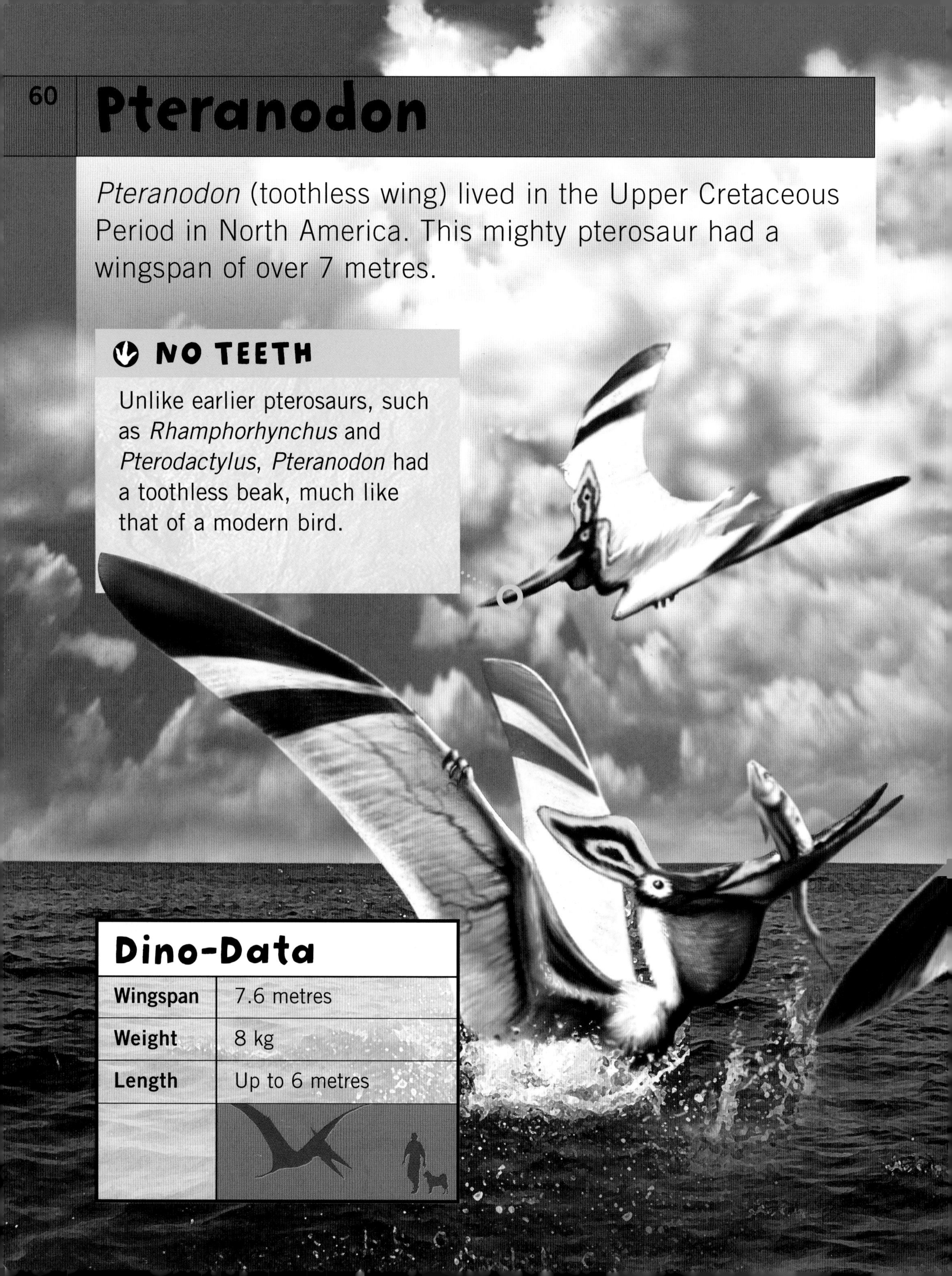

Pteranodon

Pteranodon (toothless wing) lived in the Upper Cretaceous Period in North America. This mighty pterosaur had a wingspan of over 7 metres.

NO TEETH

Unlike earlier pterosaurs, such as *Rhamphorhynchus* and *Pterodactylus*, *Pteranodon* had a toothless beak, much like that of a modern bird.

Dino-Data

Wingspan	7.6 metres
Weight	8 kg
Length	Up to 6 metres

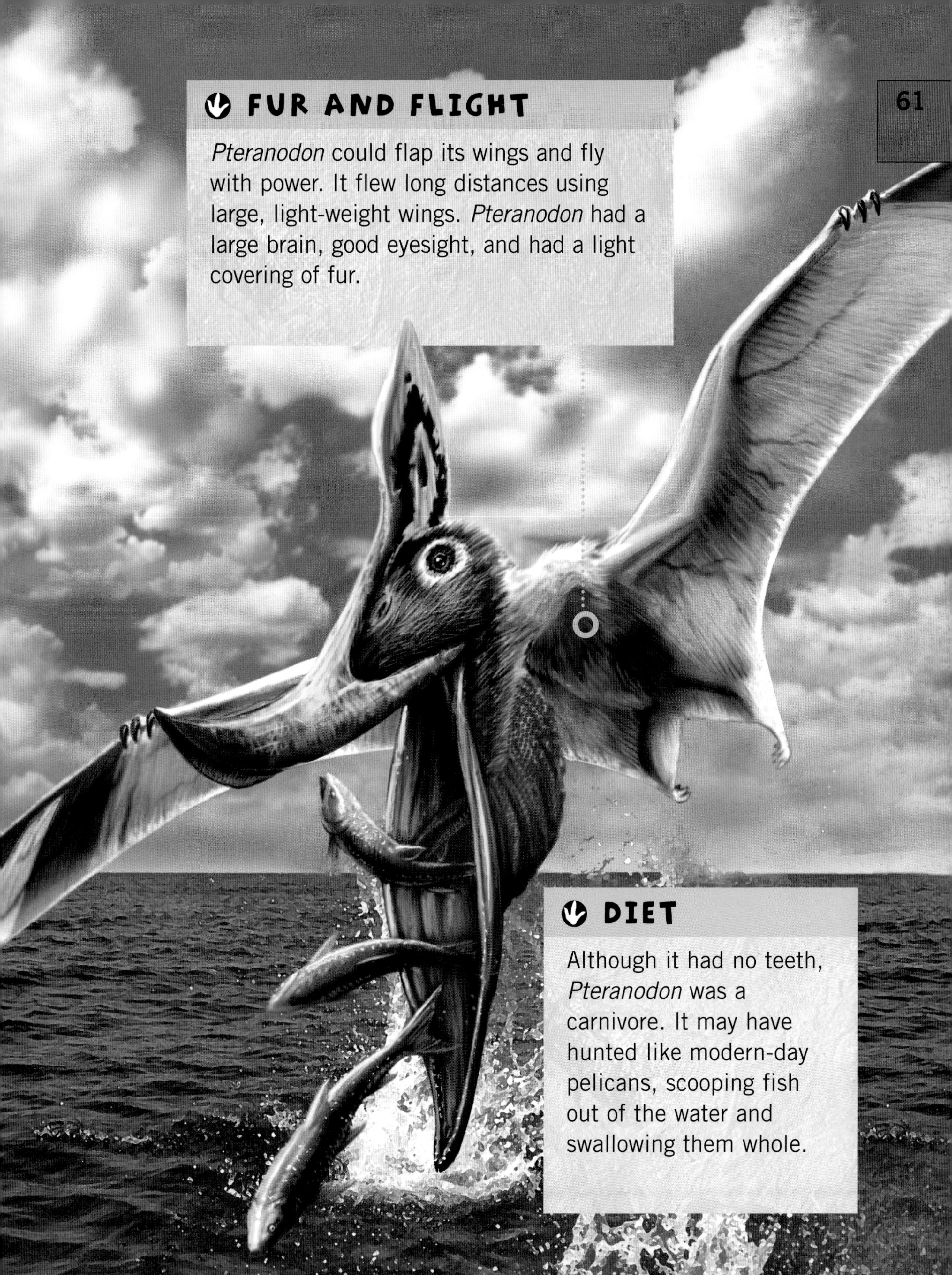

FUR AND FLIGHT

Pteranodon could flap its wings and fly with power. It flew long distances using large, light-weight wings. *Pteranodon* had a large brain, good eyesight, and had a light covering of fur.

DIET

Although it had no teeth, *Pteranodon* was a carnivore. It may have hunted like modern-day pelicans, scooping fish out of the water and swallowing them whole.

Microraptor

Microraptor (small one who seizes) was a type of small, dinosaur from the Lower Cretaceous period. Over 20 fossils have been recovered from Liaoning, China.

MAKING LINKS

Like *Archaeopteryx*, *Microraptor* provides important evidence of the link between birds and dinosaurs. Its feet suggest that it could grasp branches and therefore live in trees, like most birds. Feathers on its legs suggest that the **hind limbs** were wings as well.

Dino-Data

Wingspan	0.6 metres
Weight	1 kg
Length	0.83 metres

DEADLY CLAWS

Microraptor was a type of **dromaeosaur** – a small, fast-running carnivorous dinosaur with a sickle-like claw on its middle toe. The creature belongs to a group of dinosaurs called **theropods** – two-legged predators with sharp teeth.

GLIDER

Microraptor would not have been able to take off from the ground in the way birds do. It couldn't lift its front wings high enough off the ground. Scientists think that this dinosaur "flew" by gliding from the tops of tall trees.

Pterodactylus

Pterodactylus (wing finger) was a smal pterosaur that lived during the Late Jurassic period. It was the first flying reptile to be identified by scientists. Fossils have been found in Tanzania, England, France and Germany

Dino-Data

Wingspan	0.75 metres
Weight	0.4 kg
Length	0.4 metres

HAIR AND FEET

In 1998, the discovery of a single fossil in Germany told scientists more about this pterosaur.It had a crest on its skull, a mane of hair down the back of its neck and **webbed** feet.

LAKE LIFE

Pterodactylus lived by the shores of Jurassic lakes. Scientists think that it also laid eggs there, like modern turtles do today.

Pterodaustro

Pterodaustro (southern wing) was a Cretaceous pterosaur from South America. It had a wingspan of 133 cm, a colourful appearance and a mouth packed with teeth.

IN THE PINK

Pterodaustro is often called the 'flamingo pterosaur'. This is because, like a flamingo, it fed by filtering tiny creatures from shallow water. It may even have had a flamingo's pink colour, due to the food it ate.

Dino-Data

Wingspan	1.3 metres
Weight	0.5 kg
Length	0.6 metres

BASKET BEAK

Pterodaustro probably waded in shallow water, like flamingos, to catch food, or skimmed over the water while flying, using its beak-like a basket to sift food from the water.

BRISTLE TEETH

Pterodaustro had about 1,000 bristles instead of teeth. It used these to strain **crustaceans**, **plankton**, **algae**, and other small creatures from the water in the same way that some whales do today.

Hesperornis

Hesperornis (western bird) was a type of flightless bird that lived in the sea during the Late **Cretaceous** period. It was a huge bird, reaching up to 2 metres in length. It spent its time in warm seas, only coming ashore to breed.

TEETH

Hesperornis hunted by taking short dives to feed on shoals of fish, **molluscs** or other passing food, much like some seabirds do today. It had sharp, jagged teeth in its beak which were used to hold prey.

FEET AND TOES

Hesperornis had powerful hind legs that it used to dart through the water. It used its tiny wings for steering when diving underwater.

EASY TARGET

Unable to fly or move at more than a hobble on land, *Hesperornis* needed to be wary of predators at all times. These included sharks and **plesiosaurs** at sea, and dinosaurs and **pterosaurs** on land and in the air.

Dino-Data	
Weight	93 kg
Length	2 metres

Archelon

Archelon (ruling turtle) was a giant turtle that lived during the Late Cretaceous period. Over four metres long, this reptile could live to an age of a 100 years. The first *Archelon* fossil was found in 1895 in South Dakota, USA.

Dino-Data

Weight	2,040 kg
Length	4 metres

EGGS

Archelon laid its eggs by burying them in sandy beaches by night, just like turtles do today. Its closest living relative is the world's largest turtle, the leatherback.

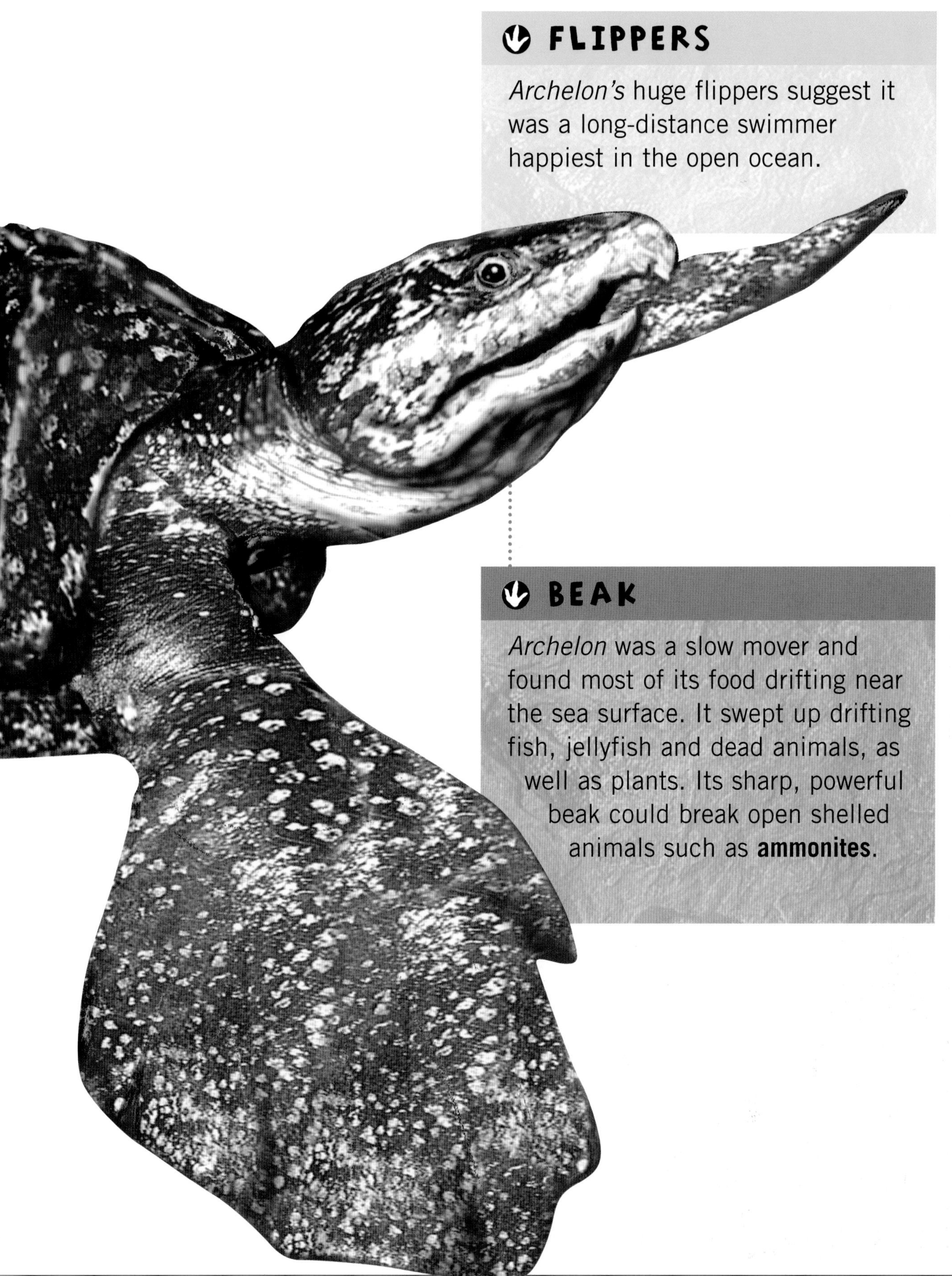

FLIPPERS

Archelon's huge flippers suggest it was a long-distance swimmer happiest in the open ocean.

BEAK

Archelon was a slow mover and found most of its food drifting near the sea surface. It swept up drifting fish, jellyfish and dead animals, as well as plants. Its sharp, powerful beak could break open shelled animals such as **ammonites**.

Tanystropheus

Tanystropheus (long-necked one) was a reptile that lived in and out of the sea during the **Triassic** period in China, Europe and the Middle East. It looked like a lizard with a very long neck.

LONG NECK

Tanystropheus had a neck that reached lengths of up to three metres. This was longer than its body and tail combined.

FISHING

Scientists think that as well as hunting in water, *Tanystropheus* sat on the shoreline and snatched fish and other marine life from the shallows, using its long neck and sharp teeth.

FEET

Tanystropheus had long, webbed feet. These were used for walking and crawling on land and also for swimming fast through the water.

Dino-Data	
Weight	140 kg
Length	5 metres (including neck)

Cryptoclidus

Cryptoclidus (hidden collar bone) was a sea-living reptile that looked a bit like a modern seal. It lived in the Middle **Jurassic** period in Britain, France, Russia and South America.

TEETH

Small fish, squid and crustaceans like shrimp made up this monster's diet. *Cryptoclidus* caught and sifted prey with its 100 long, pointed teeth.

Dino-Data	
Weight	2,000 kg
Length	4 metres

SEA & LAND

It is uncertain whether *Cryptoclidus* spent all its time in the water or some of its time on land. The fact it looked a little like a seal suggests that it was **amphibious** in nature.

SWIFT MOVER

Despite its size, in the sea *Cryptoclidus* would have moved easily through the water, using all four limbs as paddles, to swim and hunt its prey.

Dunkleosteus

Dunkleosteus (Dunkle's bone) was a fearsome prehistoric fish that lived during the Late **Devonian** period. This fish was a ferocious hunter that was unchallenged at the top of the food chain.

MIGHTY BITE

Scientists have worked out that *Dunkleosteus* had the most powerful bite of any fish, more powerful even than a shark. It used its long, bony blades to rip through flesh and bone.

SHAPE

Dunkleosteus was shaped like a shark, and was a slow but terrifying hunter. It was powerfully built and its head was protected by armour.

Dino-Data	
Weight	2,270 kg
Length	6 metres

Elasmosaurus

Elasmosaurus (thin-plated lizard) was a Late Cretaceous reptile that lived in the seas of North America. It was capable of swimming thousands of kilometres through the water using its four flippers.

NECK

Elasmosaurus' neck was much longer than its body. This meant *Elasmosaurus* could attack prey from a distance. It would wait in ambush, then flick out its neck and strike.

BREEDING

Elasmosaurus travelled long distances to find mating and breeding grounds. Most reptiles lay eggs, but *Elasmosaurus* may have given birth to live young, which it cared for until they were old enough to look after themselves.

DIET

Elasmosaurus spent all its time in the water, searching for fish. It would occasionally dive down to the seabed in shallow areas to swallow rounded pebbles, which helped it digest its food and provided **ballast**.

Dino-Data	
Weight	2,000 kg
Length	14 metres

Mosasaurus

Mosasaurus (Meuse lizard) was a snake-like sea reptile that lived in the seas around Holland during the Late Cretaceous period. It was the most fearsome sea predator of its period. *Mosasaurus* was related to modern **monitor lizards**.

SIZE

The smallest known **mosasaur** was about three to three and a half metres long and probably lived in shallow waters near the shore. Larger mosasaurs, such as *Mosasaurus* itself, were more typical, growing to sizes of up to 15 metres.

AMBUSH!

Mosasaurus was not a fast swimmer. It would have stalked its prey using natural cover provided by seaweed and rocks. Only when prey such as this *Pteradacyl* was within striking range would a *Mosasaurus* propel itself forward. Being caught in its jaws meant almost certain death.

JAWS

Mosasaurus had a double-hinged jaw like that of a snake. This enabled it to gulp down prey almost whole. A skeleton of a *Mosasaurus* from South Dakota has been found which includes the remains of a swallowed *Hesperornis*.

Dino-Data	
Weight	13,000 kg
Length	15 metres

Liopleurodon

Liopleurodon (smooth-sided tooth) was a marine reptile that lived in the Jurassic period. Unlike *Elasmosaurus*, this marine reptile had a short neck and a long head. It belonged to the **pliosaur** group, remains of which have been found on every continent.

BIGGEST EVER

The largest complete skeleton of *Liopleurodon* has been found in Mexico. Measuring up to 20 metres from nose to tail, it has been nicknamed the 'Monster of Aramberri' after the site in northeastern Mexico where it was dug up.

TEETH

Liopleurodon had a short neck and a very long jaw with rows of teeth. Because of the size and strength of its jaw, *Liopleurodon* could have held a family car in its mouth and broken it in half.

Dino-Data

Weight	4,500 kg
Length	20 metres

Quiz

TYRANNOSAURUS REX

- How many fingers did *T-rex* have on each hand?
- Was *T-rex* the biggest meat-eating dinosaur?
- How long were *T-rex* teeth?
- What does *Tyrannosaurus rex* mean?

PTERODACTYLUS

- What does *Pterodactylus* mean?
- Where have its fossils been found?
- What kind of feet did it have?
- Did *Pterodactylus* lay eggs?

SPINOSAURUS

- What does the name *Spinosaurus* mean?
- What was the dinosaur's sail used for?
- What kind of diet did *Spinosaurus* have?
- What happened to the first fossils of *Spinosaurus*?

STEGOSAURUS

- What period of time did this dinosaur live in?
- How big was its brain?
- How long did *Stegosaurus* grow?
- How many plates did it have along its back?

DUNKLEOSTEUS

- Did *Dunkleosteus* come before or after the sea reptiles?
- Did it have teeth or did it bite with boney blades?
- What protected its head?
- What other animals preyed on *Dunkleosteus*?

ELASMOSAURUS

- Why did *Elasmosaurus* have such a long neck?
- Why did *Elasmosaurus* swallow pebbles?
- How many flippers did it have?
- Were its teeth sharp or blunt?

EDMONTONIA

- Where have Edmontonia fossils been found?
- How did this dinosaur cut up plant material?
- How did males fight?
- What was Edmontonia's one weakness?

MICRORAPTOR

- *Microraptor* is the only dinosaur in this book. True or false?
- How many wings did *Microraptor* have?
- How many fossils of *Microraptor* have been found?
- What dinosaur group did *Microraptor* belong to?

THERIZINOSAURUS

- What period of time did this dinosaur live in?
- What did scientists first think when they discovered
- fossils of this creature?
- How long were Therizinosaurus's claws?

CERATOSAURUS

- What does the name *Ceratosaurus* mean?
  Did *Ceratosaurus* have good eyesight?
- Where have its fossils been found?
- What other amazing features did this
- dinosaur have?

Glossary

Algae: Very primitive plants, including seaweed.

Ammonite: A prehistoric cephalopod, like an octopus inside a coiled shell.

Amphibious: Able to live on both land and water, like a frog.

Avian: Relating to birds.

Ballast: Stones or other heavy weights used to keep a floating object, like a fish or a swimming animal, stable.

Beak: A lightweight horny structure on the mouths of birds or turtles.

Cambrian: A period of time between 570-500 million years ago.

Carnivore: An animal that feeds on meat.

Cephalopod: A mollusc that has a bunch of tentacles around its mouth, like an octopus or a squid.

Climate: The weather conditions of a place, measured over a long period of time.

Conifer: A type of tree bearing cones and evergreen, needle-like or scale-like leaves.

Cretaceous: That period of the Earth's history from 144 million to 65 million years ago.

Crustacean: A group of aquatic creatures that includes lobsters, crabs, shrimps and barnacles.

Devonian: A period of time, 405 to 345 million years ago, when fish dominated and amphibians and ammonites began to emerge.

Diet: The food an animal eats.

Dromaeosaur: One of a group of small, fast dinosaurs that killed their prey with a sharp claw on the foot.

Fang: A pointed tooth.

Forelimbs: Front legs.

Fossil: Remains or impression of a prehistoric animal or plant embedded in rock.

Habitat: A place where a creature lives.

Hind limbs: Back legs.

Jurassic: A period of time between 205-144 million years ago.

Mammal: An animal that gives birth to live young, and feeds them on its own milk.

Marsh: An area of wet land, full of mud and water.

Mate: A female dinosaur, chosen by a male to make babies with.

Meteor: A rock from space.

Mollusc: One of a group of animals, usually living in the water and usually covered by a shell. Clams and snails are molluscs.

Monitor lizard: A type of large lizard. The biggest lizard today, the Komodo dragon, is a monitor.

Mosasaur: A type of large swimming lizard that lived in the sea in Cretaceous times.

Nostril Cavity: Area in the skull responsible for smell.

Oases: Small, green areas in a desert region, usually with water.

Pangea: The name given to the supercontinent that existed at the beginning of the age of the dinosaurs.

Period: A division of time distinguished by the kinds of animals and plants that lived then. A period usually lasts for tens of millions of years.

Plankton: Tiny living things that float in the water.

Plesiosaur: A long-necked, short-headed swimming reptile from the time of the dinosaurs.

Pliosaur: A swimming reptile related to the plesiosaurs, but with a short neck and a long head.

Predator: An animal that hunts other animals for food.

Prehistoric: The time before recorded history.

Prey: An animal that is hunted for food.

Primitive: Not very advanced.

Pterosaur: A kind of flying reptile from the age of the dinosaurs.

Quarternary: A period of time from 1.6 million years ago to the present day.

Reptile: A cold-blooded, scaly animal.

Sauropods: A group of large, four-legged, herbivorous dinosaurs. They had very long necks, small heads with blunt teeth, a small brain, and long tails that helped to balance their necks.

Species: A group of animals or plants that have the same appearance as one another and can breed with one another.

Specimen: A particular thing that can be studied.

Supercontinent: The single landmass that existed at the time of the dinosaurs (see Pangea).

Territory: An area of land fought over by males of a species. The winner has the right to mate with females that live there.

Theropod: A group of dinosaurs that includes all the meat-eaters.

Titanosaur: A plant-eating dinosaur with a long, thin neck and a long, whiplike tail.

Triassic: A period of time between 251-205 million years ago.

Tyrannosaur: A large, carnivorous dinosaur that lived in the Late Cretaceous period.

Vegetation: Plants that can be eaten.

Webbed: Having flaps of skin between the toes to help in swimming. A duck has webbed feet.

Wingspan: The size of a winged animal, measured from wingtip to wingtip when the wings are outstretched.

World Heritage Site: A place of either cultural or physical significance, nominated by the World Heritage Committcc.

Earth's timeline

The history of the Earth dates back over 4 billion years. Scientists divide this time into periods. The earliest period of time is the **Cambrian** period. Dinosaurs appeared on Earth from the Triassic to the Cretaceous periods. Mammals, including humans, appeared in the **Quarternary** period.

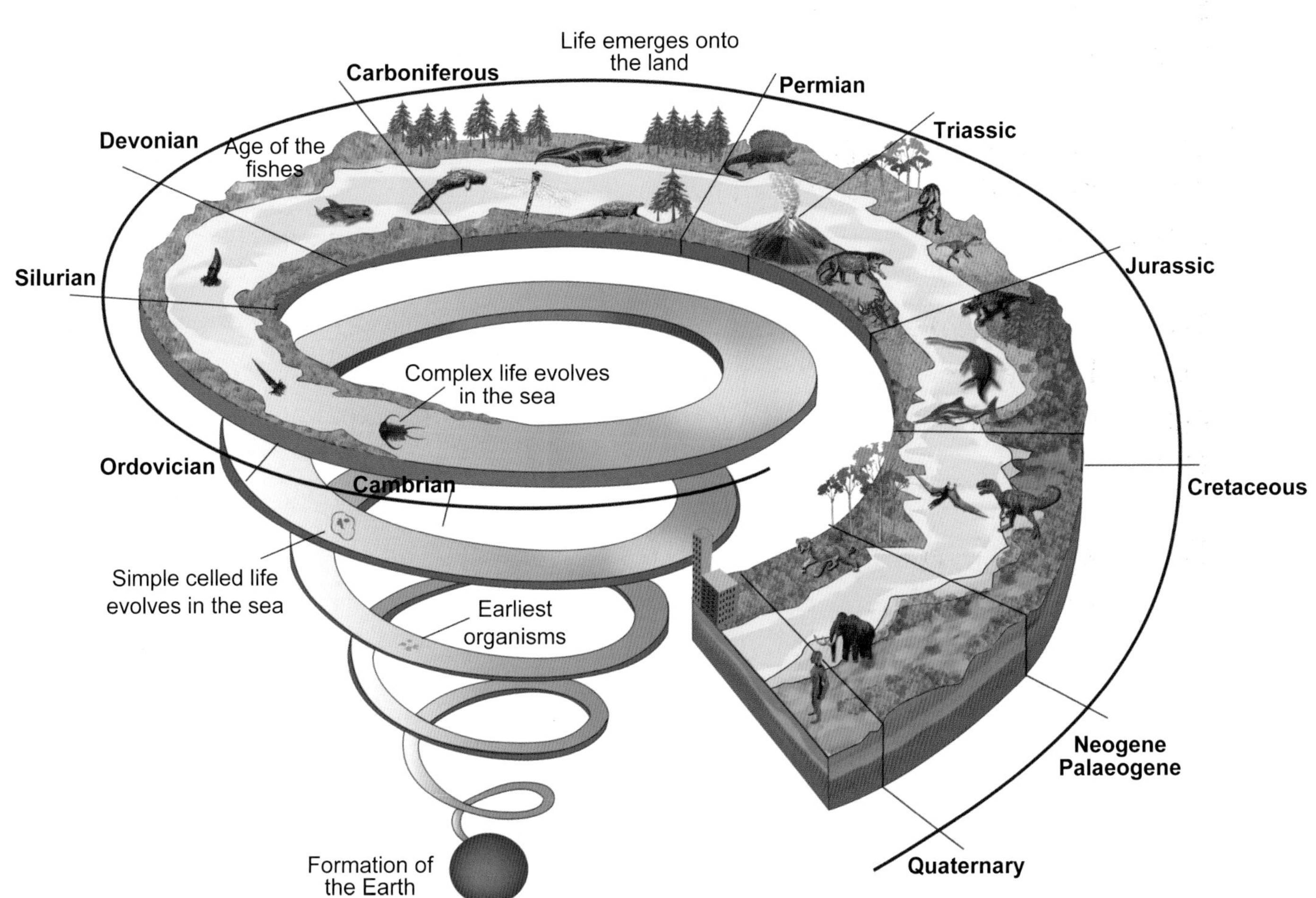

Index

This edition 2012 published by by Franklin Watts

Franklin Watts
338 Euston Road
London NW1 3BH

Franklin Watts Australia
Level 17/207 Kent Street
Sydney, NSW 2000

Editor: Jeremy Smith
Design: Nicola Liddiard
Art director: Jonathan Hair
Consultant: Dougal Dixon MSc

A CIP catalogue record for this book is available from the British Library.

Dewey number: 629.47

ISBN 978 1 4451 0967 1

Printed in China

Franklin Watts is a division of
Hachette Children's Books,
an Hachette UK company
www.hachette.co.uk